What readers say . . .

I thoroughly enjoyed *Rhymes*. The wonderful art and verse-with-a-message complement each other perfectly. The topic matter is right on target -- what every manager didn't (doesn't) know but should. *Dick Schonberger*

Dr. Richard J. Schonberger, President
Schonberger & Associates, recent book:
Building a Chain of Customers: Linking Business Functions to Create the World Class Company

I think this approach is extremely creative. . . it will significantly increase the momentum to become more people-effective in the way we manage in America. . . it's catchy, easy to read; the pictures are well done and add a lot of appeal. . . . This book has depth and a powerful message. The world of work needs it.

Earl Weed

Earl D. Weed, Jr.
Vice President, Total Quality
Komatsu Dresser Company

A very entertaining publication. . . I think this book would be excellent "pre-program" reading for managers about to embark on a management development session. All in all, a clever and witty piece of work, with plenty of pithy and important morals for the practicing executive. *Lyman Porter*

Lyman W. Porter
Professor of Management
Graduate School of Mgmt.
Univ. of California, Irvine

By Fed-ex came a booklet of rhyme
by a former student of mine.
When I read it all thru
I instantly knew
that it summed up the wisdom of time.

C. H. Lawshe

Dr. Charles H. Lawshe, Vice President Emeritus,
Professor Emeritus, Industrial Psychology, Purdue University

Sometimes managers need a break from their heavy burdens -- and from taking things too seriously. Let Scott Myers' book lighten the load -- and enlighten the task.

Rosabeth Moss Kanter
Prof. Rosabeth Moss Kanter
Harvard Business School,
author of **When Giants Learn to Dance**

This book can be a catalyst for understanding the behavior and mindsets necessary for all associates, managers, and leaders. It also provides the framework for organizations to follow in designing their own unique plans.

Mike Burns
M. L. Burns, Vice President
Human Resources & Total Quality Culture
The Goodyear Tire & Rubber Company

Reading this book was a lot of fun. Typically, managers don't read, but they certainly will turn the pages of this poetic summary of fundamental management issues and the amusing cartoons that illuminate them. Its succinctness makes for quick and easy reading, and sets a frame of reference for subsequent learning and teaching.

Harry Levinson
Harry Levinson, Ph.D., Chairman
The Levinson Institute, Inc.

Scott, you have distilled an amazing amount of wisdom into these rhymes. Of course, it's painful to recognize their underlying truths, but you have made them much more palatable so that change becomes more viable and easier to initiate.

Marv
Marvin D. Dunnette, Ph.D.
Professor of Psychology
University of Minnesota
Chairman, Personnel Decisions, Inc.
& Personnel Decisions Research
Institute

Rhymes of the Ancient Manager

Leadership in the New Age
25 Lessons Learned

By M. Scott Myers

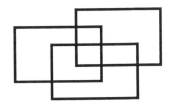

First edition

Choctaw Publishing
A Division of Choctaw Enterprises, Inc.

Fort Walton Beach, Florida

Rhymes of the Ancient Manager

Leadership in the New Age
25 Lessons Learned

By M. Scott Myers

Published by:

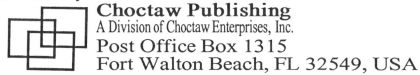

Choctaw Publishing
A Division of Choctaw Enterprises, Inc.
Post Office Box 1315
Fort Walton Beach, FL 32549, USA

Copyright © 1994 by M. Scott Myers
First Printing 1994
Printed in the United States of America

Publisher's Cataloging in Publication
(Prepared by Quality Books Inc.)

Myers, M. Scott (Marvin Scott)
    Rhymes of the ancient manager: leadership in the new age: 25 lessons learned / M. Scott Myers -- 1st ed.
    p. cm.
    Includes index.
    Preassigned LCCN: 94-070151
    ISBN 0-9639930-0-3
    ISBN 0-9639930-1-1 (pbk.)
    1. Leadership--Miscellanea. 2. Organizational change. 3. Self-actualization (Psychology)   I. Title.

HD57.7.M94 1994   658.4'09
                                   QBI94-221

Foreword

Do you sometimes yearn
for an easy way to learn
without reading tedious print?
Would you prefer to sprint
through books of many pages,
absorbing wisdom of the sages;
not dull books and monographs,
but pages that evoke laughs?

If you are that busy one,
read this book and have fun.
Written in a humorous style,
intended to evoke a smile;
also, alas, there's cause to cry
for behavior gone awry;
but within cartoons and rhyme,
you'll find wisdom for all time.

M. Scott Myers
Fort Walton Beach
1994

Also by M. Scott Myers

BOOKS

Every Employee A Manager

Managing With Unions

Managing Without Unions

ARTICLES

Harvard Business Review
Who Are Your Motivated Workers?
Conditions for Manager Motivation
Breakthrough in On-the-Job Training
Overcoming Union Opposition to Job Enrichment

California Management Review
Every Employee A Manager
The Human Factor in Management Systems
Toward Understanding the New Work Ethic
A Framework for Understanding Human Assets

Business Quarterly
Adapting to the New Work Ethic
Developing a Common Data Base for Management & Labor
Don't Let JIT Become a North-American Quick Fix

Target (AME)
Every Employee a JIT Manager
The People of Milliken
Rethinking Your Reward Systems
Who Was Allan Mogensen?
Suggestion Systems That Work

Table of Contents

Nothing is less worthy of honor than an old man who has no other evidence of having lived long except his age.

Lucius Annaeus Seneca (the Younger)
Roman Statesman, 4 B.C.- 65 A.D.

Introduction

The purpose of all management
is to manage innovation.
Perpetuating the status-quo
is leadership abdication.

Managers who bluff their way
as though they know it all,
not hearing voices from below,
will self-destruct and fall.

Managers are like other folks
who reach life's half-way mark;
some arrive enlightened,
some are in the dark.

For most it is the zenith,
beginning downward trends,
few go beyond the middle rung
in growth that never ends.

Most managers follow
the path where others go;
few take the path less traveled,
to seek the next plateau.

Insights from the less trod path
presented on these pages,
are tips for self-renewal
gleaned throughout the ages.

Barriers to Change

Folks defend the status quo
    to protect turf and tradition,
but resisters become supporters
    by helping shape the mission.

Paving Cowpaths

One day, through the primeval wood,
a calf walked home, as good calves should;
but made a trail all bent askew,
a crooked trail as all calves do.

Since then two hundred years have fled,
and, I infer, the calf is dead.
But still he left behind his trail,
and thereby hangs my moral tale.

The trail was taken up next day
by a lone dog that passed that way,
and then a wise bell-wether sheep
pursued the trail o'er vale and steep,
and drew the flock behind him, too,
as good bell-wethers always do.

And from that day, o'er hill and glade,
through those old woods a path was made;
and many men wound in and out,
and dodged, and turned, and bent about
and uttered words of righteous wrath
because 'twas such a crooked path

But still they followed -- do not laugh --
the first migration of that calf,
and through this winding wood-way stalked,
because he wobbled when he walked.

This forest path became a lane,
that bent, and turned, and turned again;
this crooked lane became a road,
where many a poor horse with his load
toiled on beneath the burning sun,
and traveled some three miles in one.
And thus a century and a half
they trod the footsteps of that calf.

The years passed on in swiftness fleet,
the road became a village street;
and this, before men were aware,
a city's crowded thoroughfare;
and soon the central street was this
of a renowned metropolis;
and men two centuries and a half
trod in the footsteps of that calf.

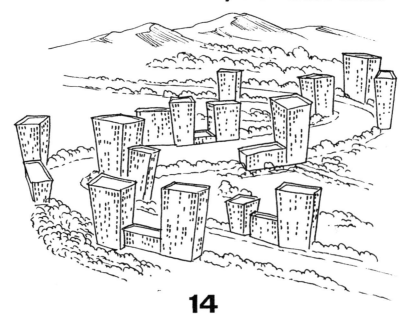

Each day a hundred thousand rout
followed the zigzag calf about;
and o'er his crooked journey went
the traffic of a continent.
A hundred thousand men were led
by one calf near three centuries dead.
They followed still his crooked way,
and lost one hundred years a day;
for thus such reverence is lent
to well-established precedent.

A moral lesson this might teach,
were I ordained and called to preach;
for men are prone to go it blind
along the calf-paths of the mind,
and work away from sun to sun
to do what other men have done.

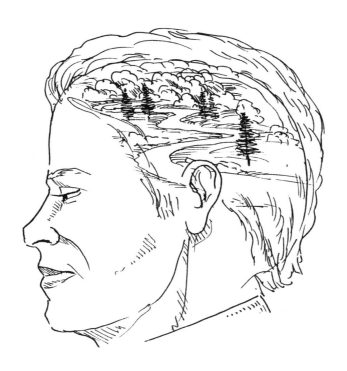

They follow in the beaten track,
and out and in, and forth and back,
and still their devious course pursue,
to keep the path that others do.

But how the wise old wood-gods laugh,
who saw the first primeval calf!
Ah! Many things this tale might teach --
but I am not ordained to preach.*

Nor am I ordained to preach,
but I quote Sam Foss to teach
the followers of Sloan and Ford
to realize they can't afford
to follow in their footsteps longer
if they wish to become stronger.

---

* *The Calf Path* by Sam Walter Foss. (1858-1911)

16

Folks heeding Juran and Deming,
learned not to be like lemming,
by following USA's Big Three,
if successes they wished to be.
Thus, shunning old trails that wind,
they listened with an open mind.

Big Three observed with sneers and scorn
new competitors being born.
Following cowpaths as before,
assured of success forever more;
basking in their reverie,
about an eternal monopoly.

But they were shaken wide awake
when upstarts began to take
faithful customers to another brand
-- consternation shook the land!
Complacent giants could not believe
their customers would really leave.

In their angry indignation
they financed costly automation.
But driven by impatient haste
they also automated waste;
failing to see that lean production
was the key to cost reduction.

Redundant managers in between
comprised an information screen
-- the absence of a common mission
perpetuated the bad condition.

Nor did they consult the workers,
who were scorned as stupid shirkers.
Union, manufacturing and design
were adversaries on the line.
Each function had a separate goal;
failing to assume a cooperative role.

Unlike competitors across the bay,
they failed to straighten the right-of-way;
but embellished the old cow path
incurring customer scorn and wrath.
Bunglers trying their flaws to hide,
only undermined national pride.

When pain of failure outweighs pride,
and cowpaths are dozed aside;
if they learn from competition
to alter methods and their mission
to form a collaborative customer chain,
world leadership they can regain.

Functional Silos

A harried manager driving home,
enjoying the rural charm,
spies a row of towering silos
on a prosperous nearby farm.

The silos bring to mind
other silos in his life
-- silos in his place of work
which are a cause of strife.

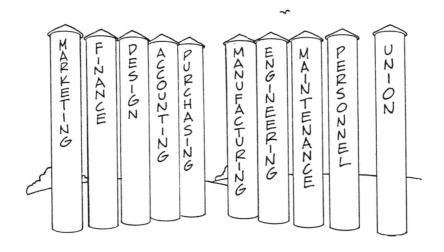

He envisions corporate landscapes
where, standing proud and tall,
silos represent functions,
each at its master's call.

**Finance ignores with regal disdain
Manufacturing with dirty hands;
Personnel bargains with Union
and its militant bands.**

**Marketing badgers Design
to keep sales prices low;
Manufacturing hustles Maintenance
to sustain production flow.**

Each silo has a culture
with a language of its own;
customers need interpreters
to make their wishes known.

Though seemingly self-reliant
and independent of the rest,
silos spy on others,
each trying to be the best.

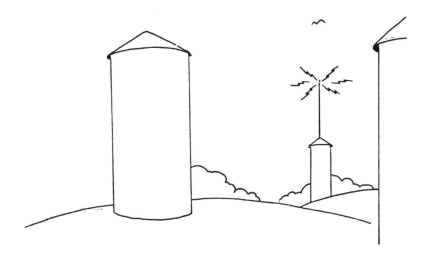

Each tries to be the first
to get corporate information;
antennas scan the ether waves
tuned to every station.

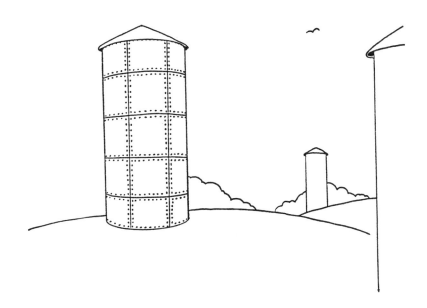

For protection from surprise
and culture contamination,
armor plate is installed
to prevent penetration.

Some use a moat and drawbridge
to control the traffic flow;
keeping aliens out and workers in
till the bosses let them go.

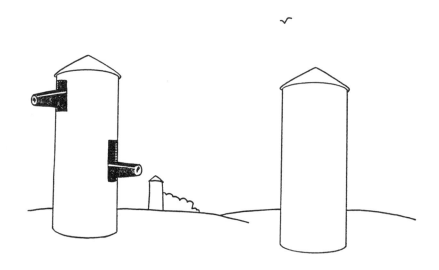

Some see enemies everywhere
and guard their home station
by mounting cannons on all sides
as a means of intimidation.

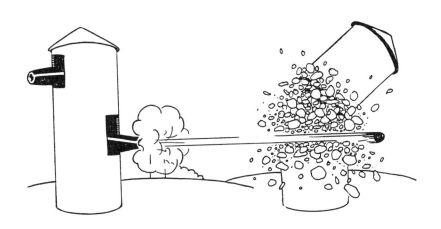

On pretext of self-defense,
one fires a destructive round;
a victim gets a mortal blow
and topples to the ground.

A competitor now destroyed,
the aggressor reigns supreme,
realizing an opportunity
to achieve a secret dream.

Before management discovers
the dead silo is no loss,
the aggressor grabs the spoils
to become a bigger boss.

Meanwhile inside the silos
morale hits a new low,
as bosses and work rules
restrict production flow.

The CEO in corporate tower
gets news screened from below,
unaware that silo bosses
don't tell all they know.

To cover their fannies,
the truth they hide or spurn,
in an adversarial climate
where few can learn to learn.

Fighting petty battles,
they begin to lose the war
when disenchanted customers
no longer seek their door.

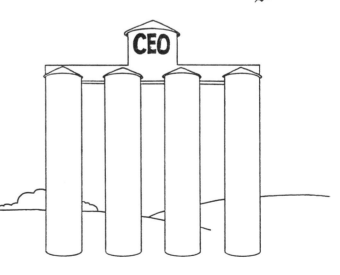

By squabbling over turf,
and building silos tall,
bosses neglect missions,
and let companies fall.

Thus, once-haughty silos,
failing the customer chain,
self-destruct through rivalry
and crumble on the plain.

Saving the Golden Goose

In days of old there lived a king
in Aesop's Fables told,
whose prize possession was a goose
that laid eggs of shiny gold.

In appreciation for its gifts
he protected it from harm;
providing food and shelter,
and freedom of the farm.

The gold eased people's needs
and kept their taxes low;
they prospered and the king was pleased
to see his kingdom grow.

If only I had more geese
like the one who serves me now,
the poor might have a better life
and smile when they bow.

He called a meeting of dukes and earls
to seek their sage advice
-- to collect gold at a faster pace,
he'd pay a handsome price.

But nobles had grown complacent
from the largess of the goose
-- more interested in spending more
than what they could produce.

A delay to hatch the golden eggs
to create more magic geese,
would take time they couldn't spare
(their entitlements would decrease!)

Kill the goose and get all the eggs!
cried one articulate dunce;
quit pandering to the goose
and get all the gold at once!

The king hesitated to kill the goose
that kept his kingdom strong;
but political cowards in lock step
voted to go along.

No gold was found in the dead goose;
poverty ravaged the nation.
The noblemen blamed the king
for the country's devastation.

As history is repeated,
a new goose fears for life.
U.S. factories are the goose
facing the butcher knife.

Bureaucrats clip the goose's wings
and plot to take its gold
to dole out to the jobless,
even though the factories fold.

The goose flees the country
to freedom and new health;
the jobless roam the streets,
seeking a source of wealth.

Isolationist political windbags
deplore lack of job creation,
blaming greedy capitalists
for unemployment in the nation.

Myopic do-gooders fail to see
the futility of isolation,
and oppose world commerce
that can enrich the nation.

If the goose is to return
to hire the unemployed,
socialistic drift must be reversed
and free enterprise redeployed.

Forward looking statesmen
respect the productive goose;
the long-range winning strategy:
let it lay and reproduce.

Little Red Rooster

Little Red Rooster scratching the ground,
looking for something to eat,
was rewarded for his efforts
by finding some grains of wheat.

Calling his barnyard neighbors;
asking for help, he said,
"Come help me plant this wheat
so we can make some bread."

"Who will help me plant the wheat?"

"Not I," mooed contented Cow,
"Not I," quacked waddley Duck,
"Not I," honked the silly Goose
-- Rooster was out of luck.

"Then I will," said Little Red Rooster,
and he did.

The new wheat encountered drought
and rain was not in sight,
"Who will help water the wheat
and assist me in my plight?"

"Not I," said indignant Cow;
brash Goose echoed, "Not I,"
says Pig, "I'd lose my workman's comp
-- let the stupid wheat die."

"Then I will," said Little Red Rooster,
and he did.

The wheat grew tall and strong
and turned to a golden brown.
"Who'll help me reap the wheat?"
His neighbors turned him down.

"I want guaranteed wages," said Cow.
"Out of my classification," said Pig.
"Count me out," chorused Goose.
Duck quacked, "The job's too big."

"Then I will," said Little Red Rooster,
and he did.

When it came time to grind the flour,
Little Red Rooster sauntered by.
"Don't look at me," mooed Cow;
quacked Duck, "Not I, Not I."

"Then I will," said Little Red Rooster,
and he did.

When it was time to bake the bread,
his friends sat idly by;
he asked again for volunteers,
and received the same reply.

"I'd lose my welfare benefits," said Pig.
"That's overtime for me," said Cow.
Goose explained, "I was a dropout
and I never learned how."

"Then I will," said Little Red Rooster,
and he did.

He baked five loaves of fine bread
and held them up for all to see;
his neighbors, suddenly friendly,
came forward in noisy glee.

"I want some!" mooed fawning Cow;
"I want some too!" quacked Duck;
"I demand my share!" grunted porky Pig;
Goose honked, "We're all in luck!"

"*No*," said Little Red Rooster,
"*I need a chance to rest;*
I can eat five loaves myself,
and don't need a dinner guest."

"*Excess profits!*" *mooed enraged Cow;*
Goose gave a dissenting screech;
"*Company Fink!*" *quacked pouting Duck;*
Pig snorted, "*Capitalist Leech!*"

They hurriedly painted picket signs,
marching round their industrious neighbor;
"We shall overcome," they sang,
"as oppressed members of labor."

. . . and they overcame.

The Farmer hearing commotion,
came out to investigate;
"Don't be greedy, Little Rooster,
you must let them participate."

"Look at oppressed Cow and Duck,
and poor Pig in despair;
and pity less-fortunate Goose;
you are guilty of being unfair."

"But. . . but. . . but I earned the bread
without help from a neighbor;
why must they participate
when I did all the labor?"

"That's how free enterprise works,"
the wise Farmer declared
" -- each can earn as much as he wants
and be happy to have it shared."

"You should rejoice in your freedom;
elsewhere the Farmer takes all;
by sharing with suffering neighbors,
you respond to a noble call."

So they lived happily ever after,
and Little Red Rooster crowed,
"I'm grateful, I'm grateful
-- I'm glad to be rid of my load."

But his neighbors wondered why
he never baked any more bread.

Reincarnation of Little Red Rooster

Little Red Rooster returned – through reincarnation,
as professor of economics, to try to save the nation.
Dr. Hilton Freedhen is his reincarnated name;
economic wisdom has earned him wide acclaim.

Unhampered entrepreneurs
keep our nation strong;
bungling bureaucrats
recessions will prolong.

Business is the engine
causing wealth to flow;
engines running low on fuel
cause industry to slow.

The vital fuel of engines
is discretionary wealth;
thus taxing wage-earners
impairs a nation's health.

A nation is not well served
by taking from the wealthy,
who create the engines
that keep the nation healthy.

Bureaucrats collect taxes
for a discretionary pot
to finance fickle spending
where mostly pork is bought.

Taxes are inadequate
to finance deficit spending;
so folks are taxed further
to finance lender lending.

The cycle is repeated
when trusting folks in rags
elect articulate dunces
and crafty scalawags.

Myopic do-gooders strive
for economic isolation;
blind to world commerce
that will enrich a nation.

Ingredients of prosperity
from which our debts are paid:
free enterprise, low taxes,
frugal spending and free trade.

E. T. Looks at Planet Earth

*A study of planet earth
by visitors from outer space,
revealed puzzling practices
that divide the human race.*

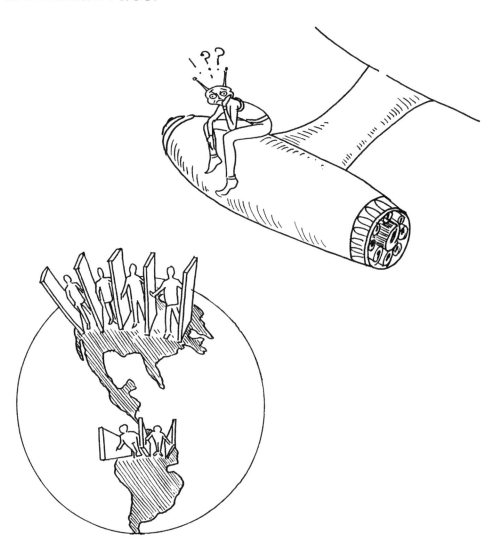

*Earthlings in free enterprise,
espousing mutual respect,
perpetuate symbols of rank
with a negative effect.*

Particularly in factories,
where teamwork is essential,
symbolic road blocks still exist
that frustrate man's potential.

Folks who work for wages
are required to punch the clock,
while salaried bosses hover near
to discourage play and talk.

Bosses park their cars nearby,
the workers park afar,
so peons' autos can't fraternize
with their master's car.

Workers wear colored hats,
supervisors, hats of white;
colors symbolize obedience,
white symbolizes might.

*An executive dining room
is reserved for the elite,
so inferiors cannot see
how piggish bosses eat.*

A buzzer tells the workers
when to stop and go;
bosses ignore such signals
but jump for the CEO.

Jobs seem to be assigned
by gender and pigmentation;
ladies and dark-skinned folks
victims of discrimination.

When buzzers signal rest breaks
vassals gulp their coffee down,
while Lords have rolls and coffee,
wheeled in by a lady brown.

Office location and access
are assigned to folks by rank;
top dog's kennel is up near God,
low dog's is low and dank.

Office space for the Commander
covers acres of ground,
while troops in lower cubicles,
can scarcely turn around.

The superintendent has a carpet
and a cushioned swivel chair;
the foreman perches on a stool
on a floor that's cold and bare.

Desk sizes are assigned by rank
-- large desks for the elect;
small desks for folks below
can't muster much respect.

Deluxe restrooms are restricted
to the Chieftain and his scribes;
urinal troughs and gang faucets
serve the Indians of the tribes.

Bosses frown at shop floor folks
on outside telephone calls;
but phoning privileges are routine
within the cloistered halls.

Bosses receive paychecks
in envelopes green and gold;
underlings get naked checks,
all the world can behold.

Fawning bosses hand out pay checks,
hoping for a friendly smile;
ungrateful wretches snatch the checks
in a cold unfriendly style.

Nor are class distinctions
restricted to the job;
earthlings are selective
with whom they hobnob.

Mortals split by legends
of immortal destination,
piously sentence others
to hell and damnation.

Cornerstones of legends
are peace and good will;
but non-belief by others
is a holy cause to kill.

The language that is spoken
or the flag that's overhead
determines who is friend or foe,
leaving many Earthlings dead.

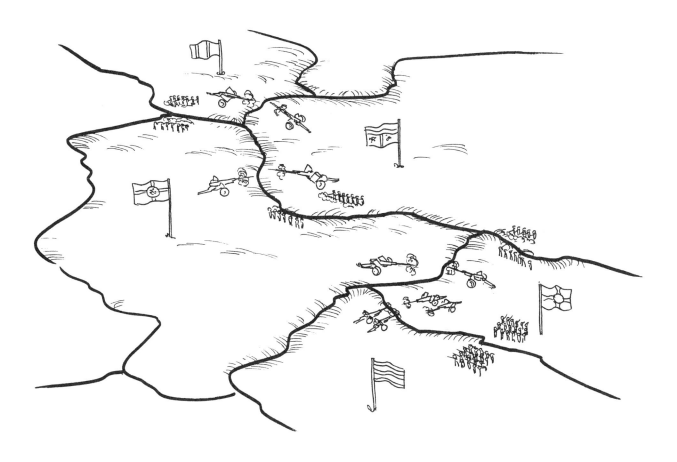

Folks vainly stake out territory
on the land where they sojourn;
unmindful that earth owns them
and to earth they will return.

ETs, returning homeward,
agree in their deduction
that class-oriented conflict
is Earthlings' main obstruction.

Relationships on Planet Earth
recall their own traditions
before emancipation
from enslaving superstitions.

Leadership

Bosses accomplish missions
by making people run;
Leaders get folks to want to do
the job that must be done.

Of Bosses and Leaders

Bosses are good soldiers
who protect the status quo;
leaders are more flexible
and let new ideas flow.

Bosses do things right
by following protocol;
leaders do right things,
however chips may fall.

Bosses use formal charts
with chains-of-command;
leaders inspire missions
that all can understand.

Bosses prescribe a vision
telling people how to go;
leaders assemble a vision
with the help of folks below.

It's difficult to reach bosses
behind their office doors;
leaders are in easy reach
on the workplace floors.

Bosses use procedure manuals
and the printed word;
leaders promote networking
by mingling with the herd.

To maintain social distance
bosses wear a coat and tie;
leaders wear an open shirt
and give a friendly "Hi!"

Bosses focus on bottom lines and goals short-range; leaders study horizons to orchestrate change.

Bosses on hands and knees await their master's voice; leaders take the initiative on missions of joint choice.

"HIS MASTER'S VOICE"

Bosses maintain tight control
barking terse commands;
leaders believe in self-control
-- empowering all hands.

Bosses are impatient
-- inclined to blow their stack;
leaders are more deliberate,
with a mediative knack.

Bosses have all the answers,
as if they know what's best;
leaders can say, "I don't know
-- what do you suggest?"

Bosses prefer "Sir" or "Ma'm"
in their supervisory style;
leaders like to hear first names
from the rank and file.

Bosses deal with individuals
with directions one-on-one;
leaders have self-managed teams
who get the mission done.

Finding errors, bosses seek
someone they can blame;
mistakes are used by leaders
to learn to change the game.

Bosses drive for victory,
with information distorted;
leaders feel they're winning
when truth can be reported.

When bosses achieve a goal,
workers are tense and sore;
when a leader's goal is won,
teams are up for more.

Bosses are slaves to process
and surrender to its goal;
leaders master the mission
and stay in its control.

GRAINS OF SAND

Eliminating a time clock
does not a culture change;
though a step in the right direction,
much remains to rearrange.

A time clock, like a grain of sand
on a sandy ocean shore,
has small impact by itself
-- big change requires more.

Footprints on a sandy beach
don't change the coastal view;
the beach looks much the same
-- sands moved were far too few.

But when a hurricane hits,
giant dunes are moved around;
the coastline has new contours
-- the changes are profound.

When the storm subsides
and its impact analyzed,
the same sand is still there;
but it's reorganized.

Hence, to revise a culture
many changes must be made
of leadership and systems,
touching folks at every grade.

Parking, dining, clocks and bells,
sir and ma'm to those above,
dress code, titles and rigid rules,
is a lot of sand to shove.

Grains of sand in a culture
are too numerous to tally;
rearranging a lot of sand
requires all hands to rally.

Cultures follow changing visions,
fine-tuned by all on hand;
cultures are in constant flux
like shifting grains of sand.

Workers get information
only bosses had before;
enabling all to help move sand
to improve upon their shore.

Rearranging grains of sand
has no final destination,
because management of change
has no date for termination.

Changing a work culture
requires a gradual pace;
but the steady turtle showed,
persistence wins the race.

Eight Kinds of Waste

*Anything increasing costs
that does not value add,
represents a form of waste
which for business is bad.*

|

Defects undermine quality,
and work must be redone;
rework adds no value,
causing costs to overrun.

2
Delays are irritants
to customers who wait,
causing them to look around
for sources not so late.

3
𝔓𝔯𝔬𝔠𝔢𝔰𝔰𝔦𝔫𝔤 is the method
by which work is completed;
if not as simple as can be,
frugality is defeated.

4
Motion is how each person
gets an operation done;
groping for tools and things
can hold up everyone.

5
Overproduction is costly
if products sit around,
to have on hand just in case
a customer can be found.

6
Transportation is the route
products and paper flow;
long, redundant pathways
make production slow.

7
𝕴𝖓𝖛𝖊𝖓𝖙𝖔𝖗𝖞 is the root of evil, stacked around work stations, delaying discovery of defects and other complications.

8
Talent is the greatest waste,
and affects all the rest;
when challenges are absent,
folks can't do their best.

Japan's Legacy

JIT means Just-In-Time
- a manufacturing revolution
crafted by Toyota
as a survival solution.

American mentors,
named Deming and Juran,
facilitated changes
in factories in Japan.

Two basic principles
underlie JIT
- a holistic process,
and the empowered employee.

People are the drivers
who make the process go;
self-managed work teams
smooth production flow.

Leaders are consultants
who advise and facilitate;
helping folks to be on time
to get things out the gate.

Components of JIT
came from the USA;
but Japan combined quality
with minimized delay.

DRIVERS
Leadership
Teamwork
Ownership
Empowerment
Enlightenment
Versatility
Security
Recognition

Each person's workplace
is orderly and clean;
maintained by operators,
as part of job routine.

People are more frugal,
keeping inventory lean;
eliminating 8 kinds of waste
while tending their machine.

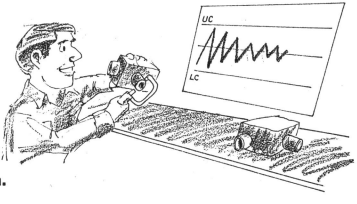

Assurance of quality
is every person's mission;
quality is determined
through employee cognition.

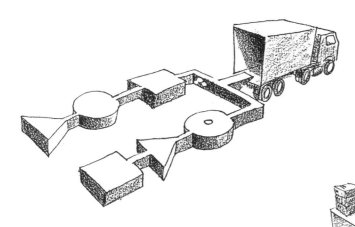

Operations are synchronized
        to coordinate just in time
for successive operations
        in a waste-free paradigm

Complex routes shortened
        into sequential flow,
to reduce time wasted
        from excessive to and fro.

Everything is visible
        on the workplace floor;
small batches make it easy
        to keep inventory score.

When product diversity
        requires setups changed,
changeover time is cut
        by methods prearranged

Products pulled, not pushed,
        through the production line
by cues from customers
        for delivery just in time.

Purchasing doesn't haggle
        to get the lowest price,
but cultivates suppliers
        trustworthy and precise

94

Each person has influence
in planning peer group work,
assessing self performance,
and chiding those who shirk.

Each person is manager
of how the job is done;
creating process ownership
- making work more fun.

Learning is continuous
for applying JIT;
work is made more interesting
through versatility.

All rewards are earned
by individuals and groups
with money and dignity
in workplace feedback loops.

JIT enables folks
to beat the competition,
ensuring job security
through employee coalition.

JIT is a journey
without termination;
each plateau is springboard
to a higher destination.

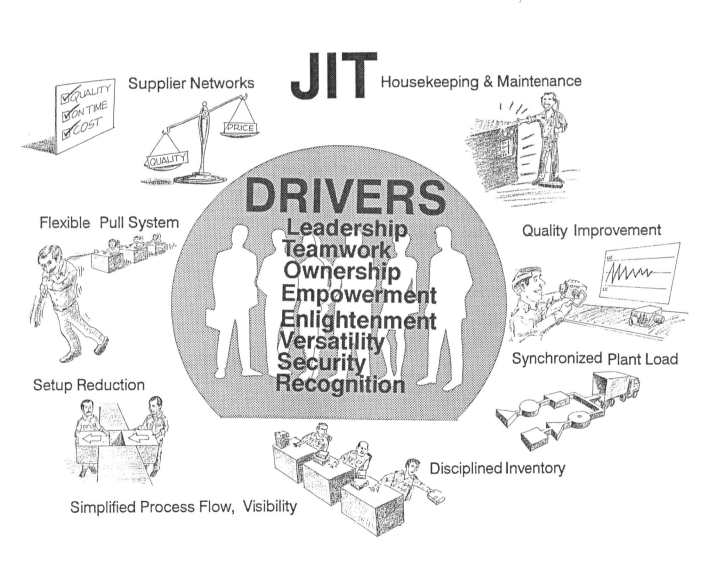

JIT

Supplier Networks

Housekeeping & Maintenance

QUALITY
ON TIME
COST

PRICE

QUALITY

DRIVERS
Leadership
Teamwork
Ownership
Empowerment
Enlightenment
Versatility
Security
Recognition

Flexible Pull System

Quality Improvement

Setup Reduction

Synchronized Plant Load

Disciplined Inventory

Simplified Process Flow, Visibility

Deming's 14 Points

The renowned ancient Guru* exhorted folks to scorn
shoddy ways of doing things -- of crisis he did warn.
To guide their recovery from habits obsolete,
14 points are offered to help them to compete:

1
Resolve to stay in business,
to be the best you can
with vision and strategies
to form a master plan.

2
Quality is essential
to succeed in this age;
product and service flaws
incur consumer rage.

3
Quality is not achieved
by inspectors at the end;
but by folks on the line
who errors find and mend.

4
When buying from suppliers
don't hang up on price,
but choose frugal sources
punctual and precise.

5
Astute management practice
helpful systems provide,
alert for system errors
to be quickly rectified.

6
Training is expanded
so everyone is skilled,
to reawaken motivation
that routines had killed.

7
Foremen and operators
handle quality control,
with leadership support
to facilitate their role.

8
Grant workers self-control
to drive away their fear;
creative effort blossoms
in a climate of good cheer.

9
Slash bureaucratic barriers
established by traditions;
let teams cross boundaries
to fulfill company missions.

10
Posters, slogans and numbers
put people's minds in jail;
let folks refine their systems
so initiative can prevail.

11
Engineered work standards
intended to set goals,
put ceilings on performance
and limit worker roles.

12
Let workers own a process
to manage with pride;
people proud of workmanship,
take challenges in stride.

13
Education and retraining
for all folks high and low,
reinvigorate commitment
so all can jointly grow.

14
The top management team
led by the CEO,
must orchestrate daily
to make this process go.

*Walter Edwards Deming (1900-1993),
Out of the Crisis, 1988.

Bosses Get Unions

Unions are symptoms of failure
- not of the rank and file;
rather, of bosses' assumptions ☞
and their managerial style.

Newly established unions
are not employee organized,
they're boss instigated
by employees victimized.

Unions create no products,
nor do they clients serve;
they simply limit boss power,
their dignity to preserve.

Unfortunately union leaders
contract the boss disease
- not heeding their members,
while seeking power to seize.

Unions are most rampant
in government bureaucracies
where intellect is deadened
by routines and legalese.

Unions perpetuate the myth
that workers cannot think,
but are simply hired hands
to handle jobs rinky-dink.

Folks on union apron strings,
when not allowed to grow,
feel they're gaining ground,
doing less for more dough.

Bosses are presumed to think
while workers do as told;
but smoldering in every heart
is an urge to be free and bold.

The latent need for freedom
finds mischievous expression
in union-sanctioned actions,
immune to boss suppression.

Organizations still exist,
not managed to perfection;
top-down boss domination
invites union protection.

Bosses treat union folks
     as if they were the foe;
union people reciprocate
     - trading blow for blow.

Thus unionized cultures
     define two social classes
- company finks at the top,
     and the resentful masses.

The resulting social gap
     creates a fatal disaccord
- rivals with clashing goals,
     and customers ignored.

Folks satisfying their needs
     by achieving customer goals,
develop pride of ownership
     through proprietary roles.

When people are versatile
     and enjoy job satisfaction,
organizers uneasily note
     unions have no attraction.

Unions are not needed
     in a well-run organization,
where all are entrepreneurs
     with peer facilitation.

When people are motivated
     through earned recognition,
adversaries become united
     to pursue a common mission.

The demise of labor unions
     is not boss discretionary;
but self-abort under leaders
     who are out of the ordinary.

The New Tradition

Divine rights of ancient kings
   were shared by association
with upper level noblemen
   according to their station.

Every person in a hierarchy
   had an authorized position;
each with symbols of rank,
   prescribed by tradition.

The king and lords were royalty,
   serfs and vassals, hoi polloi;
the role of lowly commoners
   was to bring their masters joy.

Masses born in poverty,
   devoid of information,
believed life roles ordained
   by holy designation.

As capitalism evolved
   throughout the middle ages,
capitalists built empires,
   on bare subsistence wages.

Job hierarchies were layered
   as in the courts of kings;
folks below were dominated
   like puppets on strings.

Workers formed unions
   to counter exploitation,
pitting bosses and workers
   in violent conflagration.

Companies grew and prospered
   despite adversarial strain
- all equally handicapped
   by wasteful talent drain.

Bureaucrats in monopolies
   sought few innovations,
until customers defected
   to buy from other nations.

Throwing money at the problem,
   they rushed to automation;
envisioning obedient robots
   without insubordination.

But robots can't manage change;
    do just what they're told;
unlike empowered workers,
    whose ideas turn to gold.

The biggest cost of changing
    isn't money they must spend;
it's the cost to bossy egos
    from habits they must mend.

All-knowing pompous bosses
    tell people how to go;
while leaders seek suggestions,
    admitting they don't know.

When pain of business failure
    exceeds cost to innovate,
proud bosses bow to change
    before it is too late.

Bosses in desperation
    consulted wise gurus;
who answered, "Don't ask us
    - listen to your crews."

Bosses began changing
    to a different paradigm,
entrusting people on the floor
    for quality just-in-time.

Knowledge once restricted
    to few with "need-to-know,"
is now openly shared
    with people high and low.

Companies, once proud and tall
    multi-layered in between,
reduced their paunchy middles,
    becoming flat and lean.

Leaders shed coats and ties
    that ban them from the flock
dress like folks on the floor,
    to promote more candid talk.

Rank, no longer dominates;
    knowledge and skills are boss
leaders may have dirty hands,
    workers talk gain and loss.

Leaders taking longer views
    inspire trust and innovation;
challenging the status-quo
    and folks at every station.

Employees are now managers
    of resources and the mission
with decision-making freedom,
    within the new tradition.

The American Turnaround

On the plains of satisfaction
　　bleach the bones of once-proud men,
whose successes were too easy
　　- resting on their laurels, when

Vanquished foes in distant lands,
　　rising from the dust of war,
struggled to rebuild homelands
　　to their glory days of yore.

The free people of the world
　　who brought aggressors to despair,
changed from captors to consultants
　　to help economies repair.

As humbled people tend to seek
　　their mentors to replace,
marauders traded guns for wrenches,
　　and entered the production race.

Pioneers who once were winners
    in the world production race,
are jolted to discover
    they no longer hold first place.

Foreigners are slowly gaining,
    causing economic curves to dive;
like vanquished peoples in the 50s,
    Americans struggle to survive.

Watson, Eastman, Ford, and Sloan,
    all masters of innovation,
built empires now endangered
    by masters of stagnation.

**Wasteful systems are automated,
    ignoring workers' creative thoughts;
Multi-layered functional silos
    empower bosses to call the shots.**

**Bosses diagnosing problems,
    blame others for the mess,
not knowing to check the mirror
    for barriers to success.**

Grand moguls reward themselves
    as if to prove their own success,
elevate their own salaries
    while their workers receive less.

Bumbling giants take dancing lessons,
    trying to change while saving face,
but upstarts without procedure manuals
    are now gaining in the race.

But look! - new pioneers emerge
in jobs throughout the lands,
empowering self-managed teams
to use minds as well as hands.

Skills which we once practiced
and shared with conquered foe,
are dredged up from the cobwebs
to improve production flow.

Returning to forsaken basics,
people focus on TQC,
seeking Malcolm Baldridge fame
as disciples of JIT.

Thus Yankee talent, long dormant,
    springs forth with determination;
irreverent free-wheeling patriots
    now strive to save the nation.

Giants following Ghorbachev's lead,
    shed bureaucracy's strangle hold,
pass through chaos to focused goals
    - entrepreneurs, as of old.

Convalescing giants reorganize
    to develop customer chains;
old bosses change, or stand aside,
    let new leaders take the reins.

The race is on! - but not won,
for it is an endless race;
nimble athletes at our backs
require an increasing pace.

But hard-run races are fun
with goals and trophies shared;
empowered people win more races
than conformists running scared.

A new vision is emerging
of a world where freedom reigns;
the bones of bureaucrats and fascists
begin to bleach upon the plains.

Communication

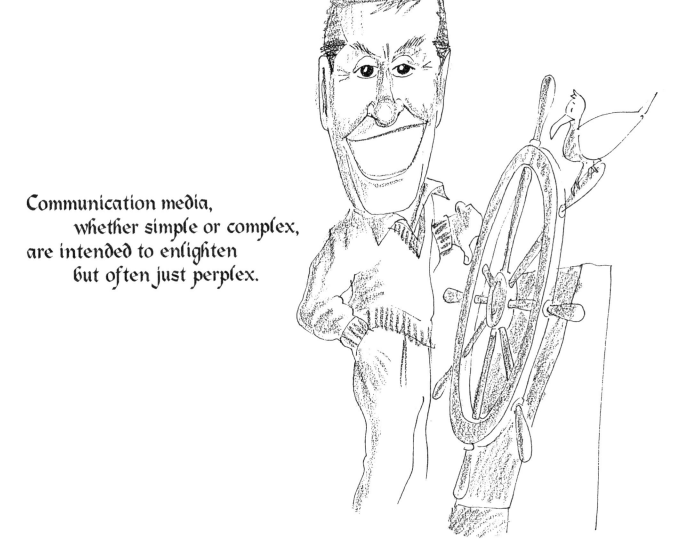

Communication media,
        whether simple or complex,
are intended to enlighten
        but often just perplex.

Three Languages of the Workplace

Words, behavior and systems,
are three languages distinct;
all three must be syncronized
for a workforce interlinked.

The language of words
- whether written or spoken,
includes formal information
and informal folks a-jokin'.

The language of behavior,
if different from the word,
even though inaudible,
is the one that's heard.

A supervisor's actions
a message does convey:
"What you are is so loud,
I can't hear what you say."

*Bosses expecting little
from folks they supervise,
fulfill their own prophecy
and don't let talent rise.*

*Leaders expecting excellence
from folks on their team,
bring out hidden talents
in results and self-esteem.*

Systems in the workplace,
as remnants of tradition,
create class distinctions
and negative recognition.

Privileges like dining rooms,
if such systems are in place,
increase social distance,
causing many to lose face.

But systems are good media
if they help folks pull together
in pursuit of customer goals
as birds of a common feather.

Three languages are essential
- just one or two won't do;
and all three must be in sync
for folks to find them true.

Programmed Paradigms

Each mind has three components
    - Parent, Adult and Child;
Parent and Adult act as controls,
    the Child is free and wild.*

Parent, Adult or Child
    refers not to age nor role;
rather, each is a state of mind
    imposing behavior control.

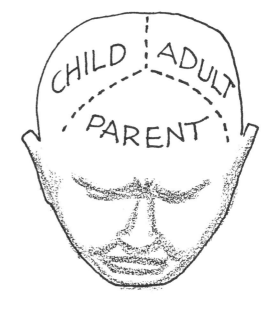

The Parent consists of values
    which to us were taught;
in attempts to shape conduct
    with "should" and "should not."

The Child is spontaneous
    - free of inhibition;
to laugh, cry, and innovate
    giving rein to intuition.

---

*Sigmund Freud labeled the three components Superego, Ego and Id. Psychiatrist Eric Berne (*Games People Play*) referred to them as Parent, Adult and Child -- terms adopted by lay practitioners of psychoanalitically-based Transactional Analysis.

The Adult is business agent
     dealing in logic and facts;
pushing aside Parent and Child
     to guide our rational acts.

Adult and Child, each alone,
     is a personality defective;
but in balanced combination
     makes us most effective.

A baby's mind is mostly Child;
     subject to Parent controls
with rules to mold little folks
     into conformist roles.

In practice, most small children,
     born with blank cassettes,
are programmed by big folks
     with logic, bribes and threats.

A child surrounded by oldsters
     hears opinions that it apes;
the values thus acquired
     are called "Parent tapes."

Programming of Parent tapes
is done by means diverse
- live and TV role models,
for better or for worse.

Parent tapes are automatic
- not requiring us to think;
but they can give us trouble
if we are out of sync.

Automatically we look both ways,
crossing a busy street;
or unthinkingly irritate others
with slurs we repeat.

Everyone has Parent tapes,
judged as either good or bad;
some permanently imprinted,
some just a passing fad.

"Honesty's the best policy,
   the customer is always right,
two heads are better than one,
   her bark is worse than bite."

In traditional business settings
   where old tapes still play,
white-shirted bosses give orders
   for blue-collars to obey.

"It's against company policy,
   write a letter to the file,
it's management's prerogative,
   give an inch, they'll take a mile."

"Real men don't cry,
   you're paid to work, not think,
familiarity breeds contempt,
   don't trust a company fink."

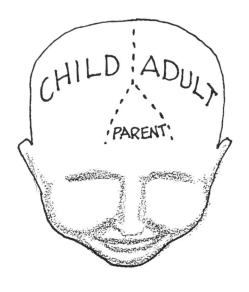

Parent tapes of any kind,
   even when judged as good,
can block creative thinking
   with slavish thoughts of "should."

Creative human beings
   who reach their full potential,
let Adult and Child call the shots,
   with no Parent influential.

118

Unintended Consequences

Inherent in the human psyche
    is rebellion to constraints;
hence barriers to freedom
    are sure to get complaints.

The upshot of this trait
    creates a paradox
-- rules meant as helpful
    become hurdles to outfox.

When tippling was outlawed
    in righteous Prohibition,
trafficking in demon rum
    became a faddish mission.

Laws to control druggies
    spur illegal commerce;
with violence and addiction
    to fill the gangster purse.

Children warned by Mother
    to keep beans from their nose,
begin stuffing beans
    as out the door she goes.

The boss's posted warnings
    to stop the baseball pool,
send gleeful folks underground
    to circumvent the rule.

Rules to limit sick-leave
    cause absence escalation,
more so than a policy
    that sick-leave doesn't ration.

Growth Management Plans
    to restrict the use of land
prompts landowner panics
    to develop before banned.

When Irish law required youth
   Gaelic language to learn,
rebellious youth in lock step
   their native tongue did spurn.

Government support for folks
   who practiced careless sex,
enable carefree folks to get
   new babies and more checks.

Legislation to help the poor
   hits the rich with higher tax,
consuming investment capital,
   thus causing job cutbacks.

Hence, fiat is ineffective
   in behavior modification;
folks do just the opposite,
   regardless of their station.

Nor is conduct improved
   with bureacratic controls;
but only through empowerments
   where people shape the goals.

Constraints are acceptable
   if the folks they command
have a hand in making rules
   they support and understand.

Why Play is Fun !
[**The key to meaningful work**]

Joe is seen as lazy
where he works all day;
but he's a high achiever
when it comes to play.

In the bowling alley
he really comes alive;
trying to be a champion
gives him lots of drive.

Why does he bowl so well
while his duty he will shirk
-- he gets no pay for bowling,
but is paid well for his work?

Much like his factory job,
bowling is a simple task.
Why not work the way he plays?
is the question we must ask.

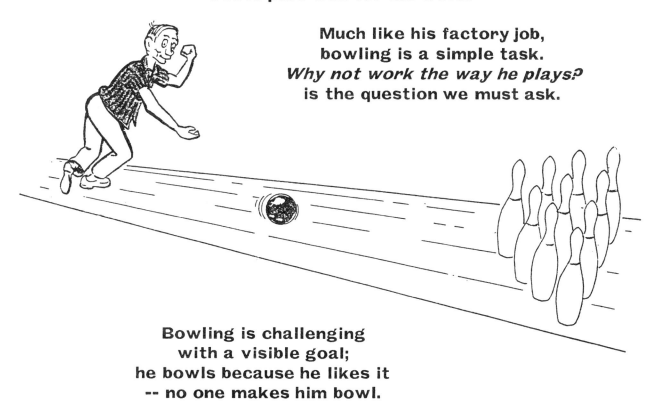

Bowling is challenging
with a visible goal;
he bowls because he likes it
-- no one makes him bowl.

Every time he rolls the ball,
he knows how well he's done;
no supervisor is on hand
to spoil all the fun.

Joe likes the competition
with himself and others, too;
and likes the recognition
from the members of his crew.

When he gets a strike,
his friends give friendly cheers;
and if he hits the gutter,
they're quick with friendly jeers.

Sharpening his bowling skills,
enjoying social interaction;
the solidarity of his team
is a source of satisfaction.

But if the game were altered
to match his factory role;
with no pins to topple,
he wouldn't have a goal.

Joy is gone from the game,
his friends are turned off, too;
no longer able to excel;
other things he'd rather do.

To keep him on the alley,
and make him throw the ball,
a supervisor stands nearby
to see he doesn't stall.

But threats do not inspire
nor sustain his motivation;
something else is needed
to keep him at his station.

"Give him money!" some fool cried,
to keep him on the alley;
but no matter what was paid
his motivation didn't rally.

He looks for opportunity
to escape this boring toil;
and finds creative ways
his supervisor to foil.

He frequents the water fountain
enjoying scenery on the way;
and makes a trip to personnel
to complain about his pay

He sees the nurse quite often
as he seldom feels right;
she is also very patient
in listening to his plight.

Frequent trips to the restroom,
two coffee breaks each day;
combined with the lunch period,
make it bearable to stay.

Some days he fails to show,
and calls his boss to say,
"I'm down with the flu
and won't be in today."

The experiment abandoned,
with pins in place once more,
Joe is glad to see the game
as it was before.

But an edict from above
makes pins classified;
a drape won't let a bowler
see the other side.

Giving the ball a mighty heave
just as he did before,
he is dismayed to learn
he cannot see the score.

He sits there in frustration;
it seems like work again;
for all he knows the score can be
anything from one to 10.

One authorized to see pins
comes out upon the floor
to give Joe expert advice
and his bowling score.

The person giving feedback
is not necessarily wiser
but Joe must listen to him
because he's the supervisor.

Joe sometimes wonders
if he gets an accurate score;
when he thought he heard a strike
the boss said, "two more!"

Sensing Joe's discouragement
and to humor him a bit,
he gives Joe a strike signal
when he actually had a split.

Sometimes the supervisor
just gazes at the floor;
not heeding Joe's inquiry
about his latest score.

Believing it his duty
to further Joe's career,
the boss gives Joe advice
he doesn't want to hear.

He continues to dog Joe,
to give him good advice.
Joe's thoughts about his boss
aren't very nice.

The supervisor boasts to peers
how in guidance he is skilled,
not knowing he tops Joe's list
of people to be killed.

Changing the bowling game
to make it more like work,
tells us why many jobs
drive the folks berserk.

Work should have visible goals
and challenges for all,
inspiring united effort
to jump when clients call.

Socializing is important, too,
as well as recognition,
to inspire folks to be a team
to pursue a common mission.

Pavlov and the Bear

Pavlov motoring through a park,
  spies a bear beside the way.
The bear looks rather friendly,
  as though he wants to play.

He stops beside the bear
and opens the window wide.
The bear ambles to the car
to see what is inside.

Pavlov is delighted
to see Bear standing there,
for he has a bag of jellybeans
to feed a friendly bear.

As Pavlov opens the jellybeans,
the bear puts his head inside;
Pavlov offers a jellybean
for which Bear opens wide.

There you go, Mr. Bear,
goodbye -- have a good day.
I'm glad you liked the jellybean;
now I must be on my way.

Bear doesn't go away,
but keeps his nose up near;
seeing those jaws so close,
the message is quite clear.

OK, here's another bean,
but I can't stay all day.
Bear takes the jellybean,
but doesn't go away.

Feeding you jellybeans
is really lots of fun;
but now that you've had two,
I must be on the run.

Are you telling me, Mr. Bear,
that two was not enough?
- that if I don't hand out more,
you might start playing rough?

Having received the message,
he gives goodies by the score;
Bear remains with Pavlov,
wanting more and more.

When the beans were gone,
Pavlov shows the empty sack.
Bear glares at Pavlov
for holding goodies back.

Seeing the empty bag,
Bear doesn't understand;
in angry disbelief,
he grabs it from his hand.

He tears it into tiny shreds,
scattering them near and far;
finding no more jellybeans,
he drags Pavlov from the car!

Friendly Bear is now content;
but Pavlov isn't there.
If the bear is to blame,
what made him a bad bear?

This story about a bear,
applies to people, too;
failing organizations show
what jellybeans can do.

Jellybean Management
(Lessons learned)

Given with good intentions;
doughnuts, coffee, and tea,
turkeys, gifts and lunches;
people think they're free.

Jellybeans become entitlements
presumed here to stay;
contagious and habit-forming
- difficult to take away.

Satisfaction is fleeting
and enthusiasm wanes;
but if taken away,
everyone complains.

When handed out equally
to high and low achievers,
rewards for freeloaders
may irk the eager beavers.

Some jellybeans required
by laws and tradition,
if treated as earned rewards,
can serve a worthy mission.

Everyone likes jellybeans
admittedly they're nice,
but for their meager payback,
some have too high a price.

Christmas Turkeys
(the original jellybean)

A factory owner named Hughes
was often in the news,
    rumored to be mean,
    though seldom seen,
because he was a recluse.

He surprised his employees one year
with a gift for holiday cheer;
    a frozen turkey he gave
    to all who did slave
in the company he held dear.

In response they said things nice
his largess was a well-spent price;
    but as next Christmas approached
    the question they broached:
"Do you suppose he'll do it twice?"

Hughes learned from the grapevine
that folks were beginning to pine
    for a turkey again,
    as they had a yen
for a turkey on which to dine.

He shelled out again for year two;
this time it was not so new;
    though satisfied,
    excitement had died;
the turkey was seen as their due.

145

Christmas three found them unified,
"Where is our turkey?" they cried;
   so a turkey free
   on Christmas three
to everyone was supplied.

A new expectation was created,
(employee needs are never sated);
   unions guarantee
   that turkeys free
each year are orchestrated.

It's now in the union contract
turkeys for all they extract
   but those dissatisfied
   with turkeys, sighed,
"It is a ham that is lacked."

Parties met in negotiation
for bargaining and mediation;
   employees now voice
   their personal choice
for turkey or ham - with elation!

These gifts intended to cheer,
sometimes evoked a sneer;
   cynics would say,
   "I'd rather have pay;
or better, a case of beer."

Gifts were of uneven weight;
high achievers arriving late
   had last choice
   and no voice,
and had to accept their fate.

Some dumped their turkey or ham
and into the box would cram
    materials and tools
    and company jewels
and rush past the guard, on the lam.

An employee was uptight;
his ham didn't smell right;
    though mentioned in humor,
    it started a rumor,
and ham-sniffing throughout the site.

To lessen bureaucratic plight,
distribution was moved off-site;
    each received a coupon,
    turkey pictured thereon;
supermarkets to expedite.

Upon arriving at the store,
and asked what they were for
    "this coupon's for you
    for which we are due
a turkey or ham as before."

The manager without regrets,
offered beer or cigarettes;
    meat and potatoes,
    sugar or tomatoes;
anything you want to get.

Thus a personal gift from Hughes,
sentimental value did lose;
    just a paper coupon,
    rules printed thereon
subjected to commercial abuse.

Intended as a friendly gift,
turkeys now cause a rift;
management and labor,
friend and neighbor,
are with each other miffed.

Turkeys give a poor return,
productivity they don't earn;
but tradition remains
with negative gains
-- an expensive lesson to learn.

Be careful what's given one day,
for it's usually here to stay;
if eliminated,
morale is deflated,
with sabotage and horseplay.

Personal

Hardware, software, and buildings
have no life of their own;
folks who bring these things to life
are the sine qua non.

The Art of Living

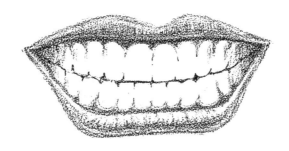

Masters of the art of living
  go their exuberant way,
drawing no distinction
  between work and play.

No matter what others think,
  unswayed by what they say;
they feel they're doing both,
  whether labeled work or play.

Their minds and bodies,
  their labor and recreation,
blend into a way of life
  of unceasing education.

They master their destinies,
  slaves not to gods nor things;
but show respect to others
  whether commoners or kings.

They simply pursue a vision
  through dedicated action;
the attainment of excellence
  being key to satisfaction.

Cages of the Mind

Few earthlings have the freedom
to give Id constructive sway;
to spontaneously accept challenges
to find joy in work and play.

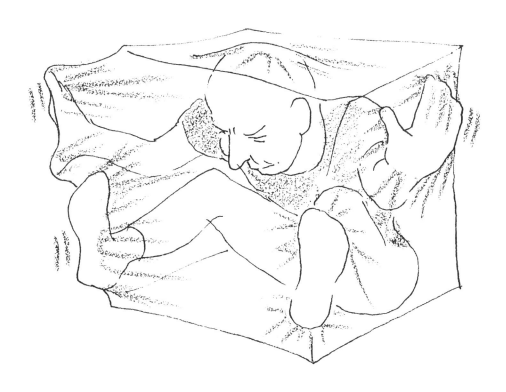

Each carries an invisible cage
from which one cannot flee;
more restrictive than iron bars
-- few look for the hidden key.

Cages, when small and rigid,
channel thoughts to a narrow lane;
others, large and resilient,
allow minds a freer rein.

Though cages imprison the mind,
they provide security;
few seek to breach the bars
to be completely free.

Hallowed citadels of knowledge
pander to man's frailty;
empowering proselytizers
to preserve mythology.

Souls imprisoned by closed minds
of smugness and superstition,
attack those whose values differ,
hoping thus to escape perdition.

Alas, most shun freedom
-- frightened sans apron strings;
for comfort, they attach themselves
to idols, groups, and things.

Free spirits who escape the cage,
dwell in detached introspection;
trading conformist solidarity
for the joys of their defection.

Life outside is exhilarating,
with freedom to explore;
uncaged minds discover worlds
hidden from view before.

Use It or Lose It

The uniqueness of humankind
is the potential of the mind.
It sets people apart
from creatures less smart,
that evolution left behind.

Though born with a blank slate,
human knowledge can escalate.
But bodies grow slowly
unlike animals lowly;
but no critter is a Phi Bete.

But critters grow strong and trim,
while most folks are weak of limb.
People's main exercise
is the blinking of eyes,
and not many folks are slim.

*Scientific studies reveal
the importance of how we feel.
A mind is affected,
by a body neglected,
directly impacting one's zeal.*

*Edison, with patents galore,
is famous in world folklore;
intellectual drive
kept him alive
- productive till age eighty-four!*

The reverse is also true;
when minds have nothing to do,
folks seek joy in life
with spoon, fork and knife,
for big bodies and small IQ.

ALL YOU CAN EAT $5⁹⁵

Folks finding life a rat race
are inclined to feed their face;
they say eating food
improves their mood,
so they gobble it by the case.

But gluttons are not alone;
as topers are also known
to seal their fate,
leaving their mate,
to sleep 'neath a tombstone.

Some folks with minds quite keen
self-destruct with nicotine.
With tobacco they reek,
too selfish and weak,
the deadly addiction to wean.

A half million die every year,
abandoning folks near and dear;
40,000 more croak
from second-hand smoke
- tobacco is killer premier!

The evolution to modern man
has roots in the primeval clan,
where the physically puny
and the dumb or loony
rarely enjoyed a long life span.

The body is designed for use,
disuse is its worst abuse;
the sedentary lout
who lounges about
is wearing a hangman's noose.

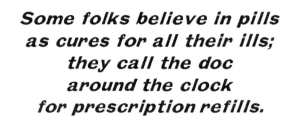

*Some folks believe in pills
as cures for all their ills;
they call the doc
around the clock
for prescription refills.*

*For bruises, fevers and chills,
they toss down a handfull of pills;
but pill side effect
if left unchecked
can create the cause that kills.*

Studies of body and mind,
show they are intertwined;
if one is misused,
both are abused;
balance, therefore, try to find.

Go for fun things you like
like swimming or riding a bike,
or take your dog
along on a jog,
or dance, play tennis or hike.

Justice Holmes at age ninety-one
read tomes as though it were fun;
to FDR he opined,
"I'm improving my mind!"
- education is never done.

Do something to stimulate thought;
find out what's being taught;
enjoy reading and discussion;
learn Spanish or Russian;
don't let the mind go to pot.

Status Symbols

Tots with uncluttered minds,
know not who they are or will be
spend the rest of their lives
discovering roles and identity.

Influenced by folks nearby,
in whose footsteps they trod,
unwittingly adapt to their molds,
acquiring their values and god.

Gingerly they test apron strings
of mentors who shape their life,
undecided to hold or sever them,
confused by options rife.

They emulate behavior
of those they most admire,
adopting their symbols of status
and to similar roles aspire.

If a role model is a sailor,
covered with tattoos;
tattoos are symbols of status
disciples are prone to choose.

In materialistic cultures
some choose flashy cars;
others adopt mod clothing
made faddish by the stars.

Mimics of Diamond Jim Brady
flaunt diamonds and gold;
others show their status
with artifacts rare and old.

Zulus had their cattle
which they traded for wives;
native Americans took scalps,
Afghanis brandished knives.

Status symbols are diverse
ranging from homes and schools
to trophies and certificates
each with established rules.

Symbols of earned rewards
are positive recognition;
but status symbols are divisive
if based only on position.

The role of status symbols
usually serves a selfish need;
to bolster one's self esteem
and cater to pride or greed.

Status symbols may conceal
boss failures and limitations,
by maintaining social distance
from folks in lower stations.

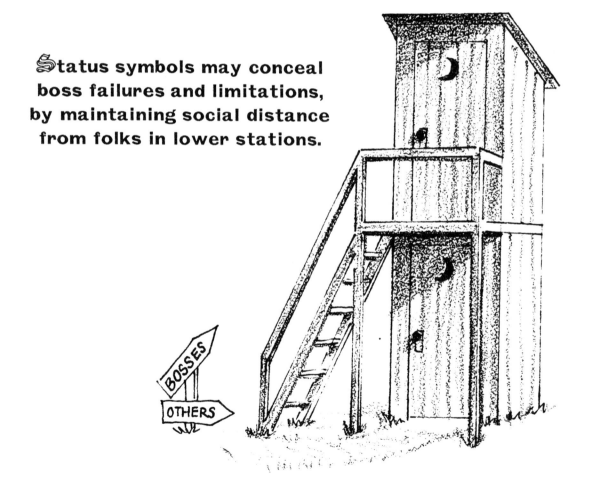

The emperor feels important
even though he has no clothes;
because subjects give accolades,
he struts naked as he goes.

Men anxious about virility
flaunt physique and personal charm
enacting the Don Juan syndrome,
their conquests to disarm.

Women facing handicaps
of gender discrimination,
outdo male counterparts
to acquire equal station.

People who feel most secure,
ignore the flock's perceptions,
flaunt no symbols of status
aimed at bystander deceptions.

Inverted symbols of rank,
displayed by people of class,
are modest hair-shirt trappings,
scorned by the climbing mass.

True status needs no symbols
to show position or rank;
rather, it's an earned good name
on which all folks can bank.

People's Comfort Zones

From birth to death in a lifetime
folks evolve through mental stages;
shaped more by experience
than by intelligence or ages.

Some move ever onward
to an existential state;
others at interim levels
more comfortably relate.

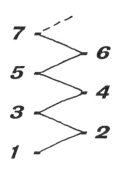

1- Reactive

Newborns have only instincts;
of little they are aware;
reacting to basic needs
-- hunger, pain and care.

Except for mental deficients,
of which there are but few,
most children before age six
evolve to level two.

2 - Security

Learning to follow a leader;
finding solidarity with peers;
superstitious and boss-dependent
to reduce their tribal fears.

As self-confidence awakens
a latent urge to be free,
assertiveness overcomes them
as self-oriented level three.

3 - Self

To hell with others, I'm for myself,
is the essence of level three;
disregarding social rules
-- willful, tough and free.

Conditions leading to level three
affect its strength and duration;
growth opportunity is the key
to move them from this station.

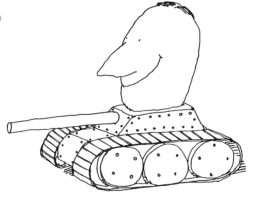

4 - Tradition

Follow rules; don't rock the boat,
be loyal to the company;
see that others also conform;
show faith on bended knee.

In entrepreneurial cultures
where manipulation is the norm,
conformists adopt new rules
-- to success patterns conform.

5 - Success

Leave no stones unturned,
do what you must to win,
bend the rules if necessary;
losing is the only sin.

When zealous entrepreneurs
have achieved material goals,
competitive drive weakens
and they turn to social roles.

172

6- People

Loving others is preferred
to winning a money game;
protecting flora and fauna
is an accepted route to fame.

But if survival needs are focused
on food, shelter and clothing,
sixes face reality
with less disdain and loathing.

7 - Existential

Tolerant of those who differ;
impatient with bureaucracy;
little use for symbols of rank,
in self-managed democracy.

Their hands-off supervision
frustrates levels two to four,
but for five through seven
it's a basis for rapport.

*Within each human psyche
all value levels reside;
high points of each profile
are the ones that preside.*

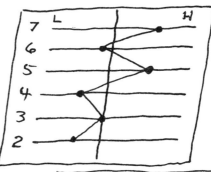

*When odd numbers dominate
self-direction is the norm;
even numbers signify
propensity to conform.*

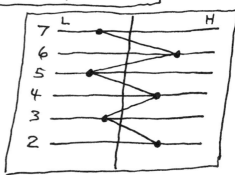

*Ideal profiles are not prescribed
- no single pattern serves all;
but knowing self is the key
to leadership wherewithal.*

*"Buy low, sell high!"**

Kudos

Teachers learn more than students;
hence I owe a lasting debt
to the many from whom I learned
lessons I shan't forget.

Kudos

I appreciate folks who can draw
pictures that earn a guffaw;
each one I salute
for cartoons astute;
but one I hold in awe.

Robert Wilmott is his name;
Santa Barbara artist of fame;
with Burma and Ollie
he chides human folly,
winning well-earned acclaim.

Don Crossley of Fort Walton Beach,
is an artist skilled to teach;
at his artwork herein
you will nod and grin;
his pictures say more than speech.

My thanks to Warren Bennis
inclitum summum genus,
whose knowledge of leaders
herein serves my readers
to overcome the boss menace.

Dick Schonberger and Bob Hall
gave help when I would call;
industrial engineers
with very few peers
on JIT wherewithal.

To Sam Coleridge I owe a debt,
and hope his fans won't fret
that I sullied the name
of his poem of fame,
of an aged seafaring vet.*

Susan Myers is a lady bright
who suggested poems I write;
her advice I took
in writing this book
-- I've learned she is always right!

M. Scott Myers

---

*The Rime of the Ancient Mariner, Samuel Taylor Coleridge (1772-1839).

Index

183

About the author . . .

Scott Myers and his wife, Susan, live on the shore of Cinco Bayou in Fort Walton Beach, Florida -- a metropolitan area of about 120,000 on the Gulf of Mexico on Northwest Florida's "Emerald Coast." They are partners in the Center for Applied Management, and officers of Choctaw Enterprises Inc., and its subsidiary, Choctaw Publishing. Susan is active in civic improvement, serving on the Fort Walton Beach City Council and the Board of Governors of the Seaside Institute. Her deep roots in the community date back to great grandfather, John Thomas Brooks, who founded Fort Walton Beach.

As organizational psychologists they have consulted and conducted seminars world-wide since 1968. They facilitate organizational change through the transfer of knowledge and skills in leadership, teamwork, communication, reward systems, conflict resolution, problem-solving, goal-setting, and culture change. Improvement processes include JIT (Just-In-Time), TQM (Total Quality Management), Work Simplification, and Transactional Analysis. Employee empowerment is achieved by getting people at all levels and functions on a common data base. Clients include 423 business organizations, 126 professional societies, 64 Center-sponsored seminars, and 57 college and university management programs.

Scott is a Fellow of the Society for Industrial and Organizational Psychology and the American Psychological Association, and a member of the Association for Manufacturing Excellence, American Production and Inventory Control Society, Institute of Industrial Engineers, and the Okaloosa County Quality Institute. His Ph.D. in psychology is from Purdue University (1951), and he has taught at the University of Tehran in Iran as University of Southern California Associate Professor of Public Administration, and at the MIT Sloan School of Management in Cambridge as Visiting Professor of Organizational Psychology and Management.

He was Supervisor of Personnel Planning for Hughes Aircraft Company, served Texas Instruments for 12 years as Management Research Consultant, and headed his own consulting firm, the Center for Applied Management, for the past 22 years. During this period he also founded and managed the Sunshine Water Corporation in Santa Barbara, California, and presently serves as President of Choctaw Enterprises Inc. in Fort Walton Beach, Florida.

Scott's book, *Every Employee A Manager*, first published in 1971, is in its 3rd edition. Reprints of his articles, "Who are your motivated workers?" and "Conditions for manager motivation" are among *Harvard Business Review's* best sellers.

Other activities include sailboarding, dancing, aerobics, tennis, swimming, gardening, Great Books Reading & Discussion, chess, political/economic (Adam Smith) activism, and catering to the whims of two Australian Terriers named Fiver and Bingo.

ORDER FORM

☎ **Telephone orders:** Call toll free: (800) 664-5667. Have your credit card handy.

✎ **Fax orders:** (904) 664-5667.

✉ **Postal orders:** Choctaw Publishing, P.O. Box 1315, Fort Walton Beach, FL 32549, USA. (904) 664-5666.

Please send _____ copies of **Rhymes of the Ancient Manager** - Hardcover ($19.95).

Please send _____ copies of **Rhymes of the Ancient Manager** - Paperback ($14.95).

I understand that I may return any books for a full refund - for any reason, no questions asked.

Send book(s) to: _____

Address: _____

City: _____ State: _____ Zip: _____

Sales tax (if any) will be added as appropriate for your state.

Shipping charges added according to method: surface, air mail, or courier.

Payment:
❑ Check: $_____
❑ Credit card: ❑ Master card   ❑ Visa

Card number: _____

Name on card _____ Exp. date:_____/_____

Cardholder signature _____

Call toll free and order now